Bill & Jill
From Federal Hill

Jill Caldarone

For Ronna Mann!
Good health & Good Luck!
Bill & Jill Caldarone

Bill & Jill
From Federal Hill

By

Jill Caldarone

Visit our website at www.StillwaterPress.com for more information.

First Stillwater River Publications Edition

ISBN-10: 0692475745
ISBN-13: 978-0692475744

1 2 3 4 5 6 7 8 9 10
Written by Jill Caldarone
All photographs are from the personal collection of the Caldarone family except where noted.
Cover design by Dawn M. Porter
Published by Stillwater River Publications, Glocester, RI, USA
All rights reserved.

CHAPTER 1

Back in the day, you could hear vendors selling vegetables from pushcarts, and you could feel the harmony they created. The sounds from nearby horses and trolley cars, ready to transport people or goods around the city, added to the scene. The weekly trips here with my family, and the little wagons we used to help carry the food home, made it the event of our week.

Providence's Federal Hill had no beautiful fountain in those days, but we did have Antonelli Poultry, plenty of fresh fish, and a 5 and 10-cent store (where Venda is now located) with a dentist and a photographer upstairs.

Things have changed, but the wonderful cuisine has not. People still come from near and far to enjoy that "wonderful Italian food on The Hill." Angelo's has been there seemingly forever and so have some of the other great restaurants.

And now about Bill and Jill! Jill was born on Tell Street and Bill was born on Aborn Street, both in the city of Providence, Rhode Island. We went to all the same schools together (Kenyon, Bridgham, Central) but did not meet until the end of our high school years. Bill had asked Jill to go to the prom! And yes, she did -- in what would be the beginning of a wonderful adventure and interesting life.

Times were not good. It was 1938. There were no jobs and not much of a future. There were a few jobs in the jewelry industry, but they were not for Bill who had too much to offer. He was musically talented, had a wonderful memory, and possessed great acting ability (as his teachers found out in high school). Mr. Grant, Bill's music teacher,

2

From The Central High School Yearbook, 1938

First row, left to right: M. Lewis. F. Greene. M. Newton
Second row: M. A, Foster. M. O'Rourke. F. Smith
Third row: H. Kennedy. M. Della Selva, J. Baldwin. W. Caldarone

"Cheer Leaders"

The cheer leaders, under the direction of Captain Parker, comprise a group of ten students captained by William Caldarone. These students are chosen for their school spirit, reliability, rhythm and ability to shout. They represent Central at all of its athletic competitions, pep rallies and lead the entire body of student spectators in their team's cheers. It is their leadership, vim and vigor that urges Central on to its many victories, and it is their outstanding personalities that promote good fellowship and school spirit throughout the school year. Their favorite cheer was composed by William Caldarone and is as follows:

Hit 'em high,
Hit 'em low,
C'mon team,
Let's go!
Cheer, cheer, Cheer!
-- Virginia Allen, '38

3

had hoped he would follow a career in voice training or singing. He had experience in many school plays and even sang in a quartet. But Bill's calling was different.

Bill's father was a barber. He strongly advised Bill to follow a career doing more than cutting hair while travelling around a barber's chair. He advised a military career.

The year was 1938. After a few part time jobs selling newspapers downtown, selling goods door-to-door, jewelry work, and selling shoes, it came time to plan for the future. Bill's first stop was the National Guard but they didn't have too much to offer a high school graduate with twelve years of perfect attendance.

His next stop was with the Civilian Conservation Corps (CCC). Here Bill became a land surveyor. A chance meeting with Bob Baillie, a fellow Rhode Islander, and a discussion of their similar unhappy circumstances, led them to hitchhike

4

their way to Denver, Colorado to try to join the United States Navy.

After three days and two nights without food or rest, they arrived in Denver only to discover the Navy office was closed. Fortunately for them, a United States Marine Corps recruiting office was open nearby. Although this did not mean much to them, since they had never even heard of the marines, they quickly decided that since food and quarters were included if they enlisted, it would be wise to accept their offer.

Bill's first assignment would be on The U.S.S. Minneapolis where he would serve for two years. "Many were called but few were chosen." This was the case with Bill and his platoon.

Bill was a mere 18 years of age and came from a family of twelve children. This new part of his life would be instrumental in changing him and his future. He found himself stationed in Long Beach, California, a place he talked about in school never realizing he would someday actually live there. The climate was very different from Rhode Island; palm trees swayed in the breeze and the weather was warm. New England had its charm, and its change of seasons, but California had cliff

Bill aboard the U.S.S. Minneapolis

dwellers, Hollywood and all those movies -- there was no comparison. But Long Beach would be just a brief stop.

New Orleans was next where Bill remembers pretty girls who gave tours of the beer factories. Then New York came after that. But "orders" were changed yet again, and Bill headed to the Panama Canal, where he spent his time in the towns of Colon and Panama City. He was reminded that this was not a vacation cruise as many a night was spent "On Duty" walking the deck of the ship and working his daily marine routine.

An interesting episode took place when Bill served as an orderly for a Japanese admiral. This proved to be a turning point. It was agreed by both those in charge and by Bill that it would be best for him to continue his career elsewhere.

CHAPTER 2

Morse Code was very important to our troops at this time. After eight weeks of intensive study of Morse Code in San Diego, Bill was sent to Samoa.

"The Rock Record" Newspaper - Samoa, 1944

It was at this time that war was declared following the bombing of Pearl Harbor, Hawaii by the Japanese. It was 1941, and this changed Bill's plans of going back to civilian life.

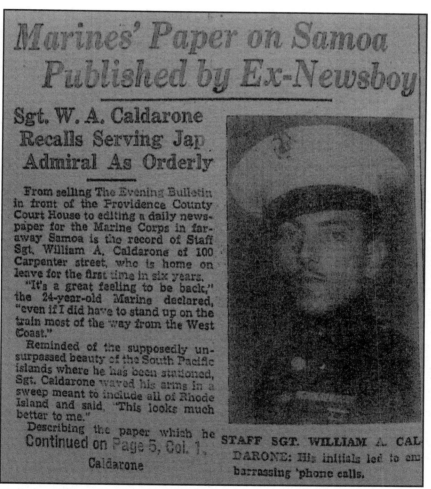

Marines' Paper on Samoa Published by Ex-Newsboy

Sgt. W. A. Caldarone Recalls Serving Jap Admiral As Orderly

From selling The Evening Bulletin in front of the Providence County Court House to editing a daily newspaper for the Marine Corps in faraway Samoa is the record of Staff Sgt. William A. Caldarone of 100 Carpenter street, who is home on leave for the first time in six years.

"It's a great feeling to be back," the 24-year-old Marine declared, "even if I did have to stand up on the train most of the way from the West Coast."

Reminded of the supposedly unsurpassed beauty of the South Pacific islands where he has been stationed, Sgt. Caldarone waved his arms in a sweep meant to include all of Rhode Island and said, "This looks much better to me."

Describing the paper which he

Continued on Page 5, Col. 1.

Caldarone

STAFF SGT. WILLIAM A. CALDARONE: His initials led to embarrassing 'phone calls.

From the Providence Journal-Bulletin

In Samoa, Bill started a newspaper called *The Rock Record* which provided the troops with a way get and read the news. He utilized Morse Code as his language of choice and he used a hand cranked mimeograph machine for printing.

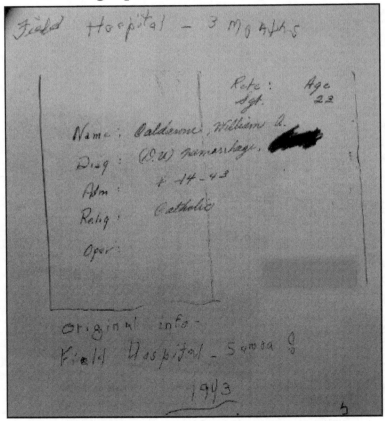

Medical report from a field hospital in Samoa.

CHAPTER 3

In 1944, after two years in Samoa, Bill was transferred to Camp Lejeune, North Carolina. Here he was put in charge of teaching Morse Code and he established a new standard procedure for teaching code at all USMC Code schools. During this period of travel and learning, he always hoped he would be stationed closer to home. Family and friends had suddenly come back into focus and life was becoming more involved.

I had not heard much from Bill while he was away, but suddenly one day, there he was. We had a surprise meeting on the street. He was on his way to visit my house when I noticed a person in military attire approaching me. Since he had just returned from the tropics, he found Rhode Island was too cold, and his collar was tightly wrapped around his cheeks keeping his face out of view. I found myself suddenly wrapped in his arms -- all I could do was guess that it was Bill. My plans for that evening suddenly changed.

Bill's face was tan and he was no longer that high school graduate who once took me to the prom. And also gone were the days that he spent in San Diego on leave, taking lovely ladies to dances and doing the *San Diego Hop*. From what I heard he had been quite the star!

After spending a few days at home recuperating from the climate change, he returned to the base at camp. Our correspondence became more intense and his visits back to Rhode Island became more frequent. He was very popular with my friends in the Navy Shipyard at Quonset where I worked in the confidential department for the government. It seems that his occasional appearance in his dress blues and the "one rose" he brought for me was what all our group waited for -- he did make a handsome marine. This lifted the spirits of my office help, too, since most had friends and relatives in the military fighting a war in faraway places.

I tried to do my work but also make time for him. It was announced one day that if we gave a blood donation for the boys "over there" we could have the afternoon off . Of course I gave my blood for a good cause. And then Bill and I left and had a lovely afternoon together at Roger Williams Park. It was not long after that he proposed marriage.

It was 1944 and the war was still on. My sister had just married six months earlier, and I was concerned that my mom would be left alone if I married, too. However, we still decided to go forward with our plans to marry.

It was not easy. We had no formal wedding invitations and NO TIME as Bill was on leave for only a few days. With the help of family and friends we were still able to arrange a church wedding. My sister made the wedding cake, my mom and others helped with food, we used the phone to invite our friends, the church came available -- and it was done!

CHAPTER 4

I t is now time for a little update about Jill -- that's me!

The year was 1938 and I was working at a jewelry store in downtown Providence. In September of '38, we experienced a hurricane -- *The Great Hurricane of '38*. This was most uncommon years ago and the city had no hurricane barrier at the time. Consequently, the downtown area of Providence became completely flooded. We stayed in the store until the water seeped under the closed doors and rose to reach almost shoulder height, then we were forced to evacuate. It became worse when the watch repairman's chemicals started to spill into the water. We had to form a human chain to get out of the area, and it was most difficult to walk against the current and get access to the nearby Alice Building for protection.

The Great Hurricane of 1938,
Jamestown Beach, RI
(courtesy Rhode Island State Archives)

With no communication and no electricity, we had no way to notify our folks at home. After a very distressing night, we heard voices and discovered people walking outdoors. The floodwaters had receded, but the damage to all the buildings was very bad. We were thankful to have our lives but I was saddened to learn about the loss of my family's beach home on the waterfront.

Many people were killed during the storm which was so bad that houses floated across Narragansett Bay. Eyewitnesses told us that our house and garage were picked up by one wave, and a second wave tossed them into the bay. This staggering experience along with happenings of the time -- such as our nation's recovery from The Great Depression and then the surprise attack by the Japanese at Pearl Harbor -- made our generation very weary.

Truly amazing is the fact that not only were we such a young country (most of us had first generation parents who were immigrants from their native country not long before) we somehow emerged from all this stronger. Tom Brokaw did say that we are part of the "Greatest Generation." How true!

After a succession of different jobs, which were mostly office work in credit departments, I tried something different. I went to work in a plant that made artificial flowers. It was truly a delightful experience. The owner started his business the hard way -- by selling apples on the street corner to earn money. It was in this way Mike D'Agnillo founded the California Artificial Flower Company. He created some of the most beautiful flowers found anywhere in the world. His company thrived until other countries started competing with cheaper help. His building still stands today as evidence of his work, but void of all the flowers; divided spaces for different businesses now occupy the building. We miss our yearly Calart business outings to Block Island on the local excursion boat. Mike was noted for having lovely employees because he believed the girls enhanced the beauty of his business.

My school training was put to good use when I went to work for the Gladdings Company in downtown Providence, a most respected and reputable department store. Little did I know that when I was hired they needed someone to help them in the credit department, and here I was surprised to find an addressograph and a graphotype machine that was very much in disarray and in need of help. These machines were used to print monthly statements for billing purposes. I do not know how long they had not been used, but it seemed like there had been much neglect.

I worked very hard lining up the print and threading it through the machines to bring them to date. The customers metal name plates had to be hand-fed into the addressograph for printing.

This job went well until I decided 1 wanted to help with our government's effort at The Quonset Naval Base where ships were being built for the war. My work in Quonset involved handling much confidential data that had to be distributed properly to individuals. My co-worker was from the South; a lovely young lady whose husband served in the Navy nearby.

This brings me up-to-date, except that while the men were all away fighting the war, we women were trying our best to survive and keep the home front going. Between daily visits to the church, dances that were properly sponsored (by the CYO or Rhodes on the Pawtuxet), lots of walking (there were no cars), and taking buses to beaches or parks, we tried to convince ourselves that soon the war would be over. The news from the war was especially tragic. So many of our young men and women were dying. Months later, I would see for myself the oil seeping out of the ship that was sunk at Pearl Harbor with 1,100 men onboard; so final, and there it was -- ship oil and memories. I would never forget it. Yes, after we married, Bill and I lived in many different places. Hawaii would be one of them.

We of that generation cannot easily forget these times. Gas was rationed along with many food items and even women's stockings were collected since the material used had to be reallocated for the war effort, along with so many other common items. Somehow the sadness and concern of the times was helped by the wonderful people who traveled to entertain the troops. Bob Hope was one big attraction. The Big Bands of the day helped to keep us all mentally stable. Many of the songs popular at the time were sad like *I'll Never Smile Again*. So memorable and so great.

Time passed, and Bill finally came home.

CHAPTER 5

Yes, we were married on August 21, 1944. It was a great day and very warm. Many friends and family attended our quickly arranged wedding. The priest was happy since he had known both of us from an early age.

We did not have much time since Bill had to be back at camp in a couple of days, so we stayed at the Biltmore for just one night. And the very next day we were on the train heading for North Carolina!

This was quite a quick change for me. The war was still on, and I did not even know that Bill had arranged for us to stay at a camping lodge. He had told me we might not have a place to stay,

From The Providence Evening Bulletin

however, his buddy was able to arrange for us to rent the lodge for the time being.

I remember that the train trip was awful. Military men had priority, so we had to sit on our suitcases most of the way. We made one overnight stop before arriving, and there was no air conditioning.

We finally made it to Camp where Bill's buddy met us and brought us to our camping lodge. It was located along the inland waterway and was just lovely. Conveniences were few -- there was no indoor plumbing and we had to walk to the outdoor "john," well water had to be pumped, there was an "ice box" with no refrigeration, and we only had a kerosene stove for cooking. But considering the alternatives, this was heaven.

My life as Mrs. William Caldarone had now begun.

Our first home -- A hunting lodge
on the inland waterway, North Carolina.

A new life and a new name -- and indeed, a name that gave great dignity to our new family. The Caldarones originally came from Spain. From there they went to Italy, settling in the Province of Caserta, in the municipality of Marzano Appio. Angelo was Bill's grandfather and he was born in the city part of the village. My father Martino just happened to be born in the same area -- how about that!

Upon arriving in America, the Caldarones were the first to start a bank on Federal Hill in Providence to help newly arriving immigrants.

So here I am with a new name and living in a strange area -- part of the first military family to live at this location. My first impression was that they were a wonderful people to accept me as one of their own. First of all, I talked different -- but so did they! They did not seem to know much about our clams or quahogs. And I did not know much about their southern fish frys, the different greens that were growing in their gardens, or about the many peanut and tobacco fields. I was also very apprehensive about the chiggers, ticks and snakes.

My neighbors Nel and Nathaniel were great. They introduced me to many of the Southern ways. My days were spent either decorating my little house, trying to cook on a kerosene stove, learning more about the South, or waiting to see my husband walk home from the corner where he was dropped off each day. No we did not yet have a car.

As days grew into months, I slowly became accustomed to the strict routine and atmosphere on the base. It was still wartime and restrictions were many. Shopping at the commissary and the PX was intimidating at first. Never had I been surrounded by so many strangers in military uniforms. The wives were great; we all tried to help each other.

Now it was time for me to learn how to drive. Bill managed to find a used car and used our wedding gift money to purchase it. Yes, he drove it home one day and we were so happy. But driving in that area was not easy as there were no paved roads. If you managed to stay in the tracks on one of the silky, dusty roads, then all was well. But if you took a wrong turn, you would be in a ditch. And yes, that's exactly what I did! And alongside the ditch was a field full of hogs -- they were big pigs and not friendly. Bill said that since I put the car the ditch, it was up to me to get out.

Our first car!

After shedding a few tears, I conquered the roads. It was something I will never forget. The car was behaving nicely until one day nothing happened -- it wouldn't start. Low and behold, Bill did not know he had bought a car with a cracked block.

Time was fleeting -- the rumor was that Bill and the others would be shipped out soon. We had to get the car fixed. We found a mechanic who let us use a wristwatch for collateral and allowed me to take the car back home to Rhode Island. Those last days together were frightening, since I could not drive the car and also was pregnant. Then suddenly Bill was gone, sent off to China this time -- a horrible feeling. I thank Nel and Nathaniel who helped me through that terrible time. But it was time for me to leave, too. That car with a cracked block would not be stopped.

My trip home in that car would not be safe, but a fellow marine volunteered to drive it. I had no choice. We drove all the way to Rhode Island without once stopping. Yes, we made it, and the "wonderful dream" of a car then stood in the back yard until Bill got home to dispose of it later.

During the time that I was in Willis Landing, North Carolina, we had many interesting things happen. During the first few days at our campsite I heard strange bumping sounds under the house. Low and behold, I did not know that the families nearby were raising pigs. The cute little piglets would get out of their enclosed areas for their morning run. This is what we were awakened to: "*Oink, oink... here, here!*" which combined with the noise on our tin roof when it rained. It wasn't too bad until one day one of those big ornery hogs decided he did not want to get castrated. I heard people shouting, "*stand by!*" Since I happened to have a broom in my hand at the time, I thought I could stop him with a swat. Needless to say my broom handle broke and the hog kept running.

Another wonderful activity is cooking a turkey on a stove fueled by kerosene. And it was a success!

It was also great to have the property owners pay us a visit. We had never met them since they allowed our neighbors to take care of the property. Of course my door was locked and they were not allowed in until I was told who they were. It was one of the best things to have ever happened. They were from Greensboro and were such wonderful people. I enjoyed the misses' Southern cooking, especially the chicken and dumplings.

I recall another memorable cooking experience. It was a rainy, muddy day and I decided to make a nice Italian dinner for my neighbors. Since l could not bring many clothes with me from home, I wore some of Bill's dungarees. Well dinner was ready and when it came time to deliver, I had to put on Bill's long rain coat because of the weather. All was fine until I stepped outside and slipped in the mud. There I sat with muddy spaghetti and meatballs all around me. All I could do was sit and cry. Seems like I shed a few tears at that place. I guess it was all part of the new experience.

Another memory comes to mind. It was August of 1944. The weather was warm when we arrived in our quaint little area. I learned to watch for the fish as they were swarming in anticipation of the fish frys. The few families that lived there, who were all related, also had chickens roaming around. I thought it would be great if I could let my recently acquired little chick run around with theirs. Yes, I got the OK.

However, much later when the chick was grown, and it would have made good eating, I could not find it. Much to my disappointment, I had to accept an Old Hen in place of my Spring Chicken. The Old Hen really did not want to cooperate. When it was time to prepare her for eating, someone tried to decapitate it and succeeded except the Old Hen decided she wasn't ready. She took off! Since the houses had no foundations, we were all looking under all of the houses for this poor little thing running around with no head. Yes, we finally did catch it. But now I know what is meant by people running around "like a chicken with their head cut off." It was funny and yet sad. I do not recall if we really enjoyed eating it or whether we ate it at all. It was a tough ol' bird.

As the weather turned colder, my Southern friends were making sure that I was shown all the area including the smoke houses for the tobacco. The tobacco was brought to auction houses. Quite interesting to see them bid. A famous quote after bidding, "*Hang that one on the line, K?*"

October came too quickly. Bill was gone. I had to get home. Before I left, I spent a brief time in the hospital because doctors wanted to be sure I was not going to lose our baby. As I look back to all the happenings and the wonderful Southern hospitality, it all seems so impossible. How could I ever forget it?

Now I came back to Rhode Island and back to reality. Thankfully I was able to live with my mom until I had my baby. Bill was sent to California and then to Guam. My first son was born in July of '45' and Bill was told of his son while he was in Guam. From there he was sent to China. Thankfully the war was over in 1945 shortly after our first son was born.

During this time I had arrived back in Rhode Island, and having a child without his father around was not easy. The women from this era did not have as much help as they do today. There were times when the men would be called to duty at night and we women were left to fend for ourselves. I believe we were called "Grass Widows" but somehow we helped each other and survived. I remember trying to save some things for Daddy to see, liking not wanting our son to walk until he came home. Yes, he did walk for Dad when he was one year-old.

Our next stop was Quantico, Virginia. Bill was in charge of the equipment board and he also taught Morse Code. This was a great place -- the weather was good, and the base did not seem so intimidating. And this is where our second son was born. Wow, things were different now -- two boys!

Dumfries, Virginia would be next. Our little house here was conveniently close to the base. It had just two small bedrooms, an open kitchen and a family room with a potbellied stove. At this time, we were quite happy to have our first television (which was still a novelty and not fully perfected yet). The pictures did not "hold" -- they would roll -- but we were still so happy to have it.

Our home in Dumfries, Virginia.

Then one day, the stove started to overheat and made a terrible roar with smoke. Needless to say, the evacuation from our house was quick. The TV was saved first, and the family came later. We never did find out the cause of this problem, we were just happy to leave that place safely.

Our stay in Virginia was quite eventful for the family, especially for the boys. The area was significant in the founding of our young country, and featured important historic areas like Manassas (where two Civil War battles were fought), the Blue Ridge Mountains, and Washington itself which was only about 30 miles away. Frequent sightseeing trips were made. It was also eventful because my second son was born at Quantico on the marine base. However, our next stop would be much better than all the others.

CHAPTER 6

Now I am talking of HEAVEN. Yes, HAWAII! What a wonderful way to end a career!

The boys were now old enough to enjoy different things like scouting, hiking and swimming. Out of necessity, I became a Den Mother for the local Cub Scouts. It was a great experience. All our den's achievements were recorded, and once a year we would have the annual *Makahiki* in Oahu, which meant that all the scouts from Oahu would gather at a place near Honolulu where they would be recognized for their achievements.

And while all this was happening, I somehow found that my personal interests were drawing me toward the plant world.

Jill with Cub Scout Den #4, Kailua, Hawaii

When we lived in California, I had met people who were studying the Art of Bonsai, a style of gardening of Japanese origin. I became very interested. Since I have always enjoyed working with plants, this extension of gardening was easy for me to follow.

I learned a few chords on the ukulele and of course we all tried the hula. We all felt fully immersed in this way of life until I had a rude awakening again -- housing. When we first landed in Oahu, it was so wonderful seeing the palm trees, feeling the warm breeze, and smelling the pineapple in the air. Oh how great! Our first night on the island was at a motel called the Thaliana alongside the canals.

A story from the Honolulu Star-Bulletin, 1957.

CHAPTER 7

We were transferred to Great Lakes, Illinois. From warm and sunny to harsh cold winter in and near Chicago. Not good. First of all, military families were not welcome so finding housing was very difficult. I tried placing an ad written in Italian in the local newspaper hoping that maybe someone in the Italian neighborhoods would accept us -- especially since our family had two little boys. Thankfully, a friend of Bill's, Buddy Rosindo, took us in until we could find our own housing. This was an acceptable arrangement even though it meant living in just one bedroom while Bill tried to get us closer to his school in Great Lakes, near Chicago, where he trained.

We had only a cold water flat-kerosene stove for heat, there was mold half way up our walls, both of our kids got sick, and Ron contracted pneumonia. I finally had to bring the kids home to Rhode Island. But not too long after that, Bill called to say we were transferred again -- this time to California. Oh, Happy Day!

It was great to know that Bill would have better duty and the climate would be much warmer. However, since housing was always a problem, we felt fortunate to be told that housing would soon be available. This was good news since the motels were not always a desirable place for little children to live. One of the "houses" we lived in here in California was an abandoned ranch that had lovely avocado and fruit trees, but it was filthy. This would be OK for a while. Then finally, we were told that the base housing was available and we moved.

Considering what we had, this should have been great. And it was great until a sandstorm hit us in our new Quonset Hut! Needless to say, it was not easy to keep the sand out. And as a result, our youngest son got pneumonia again! But somehow we survived this, too... and on to our next stop: we were heading back to camp, North Carolina.

Quonset Huts at Camp Pendleton, California.

This wasn't too bad a move as we were able to get brand-new base housing. The boys were older now, and they even helped Mom wash the car when Dad was away on maneuvers. This was my second time at this base. The first time had been as a new bride, and now I returned as a mother of two. There was much to do here, since the boys were at school, Richard was a Cub Scout, and I was helping out with church work.

I had also been going into areas that were "no-no's" at the time. As a Northerner, I was very naive about racial stuff. Down South it was different. To me, people are people. But l was warned not to do certain things, like to put leaflets at the train station only in the White areas and not the Black. It was too bad, however I do hope that things have changed since I was there.

Once we stopped in an area and Mrs. H. warned me not to venture out of the car. It was an emergency stop, and the people all knew Mrs. H., but not me. She was safe but I wasn't. I was happy when she reappeared with what she needed and we got out of there.

CHAPTER 8

Our next stop was Hawaii again. This was heaven. One night after the boys were put to bed and were safe, we decided to venture out the door to enjoy the night air. Little did I know that one of the big frogs from the water area was "croaking" around the motel. They were having a good time jumping around, not knowing that we would be in their path. Suddenly, I felt this thing strike me in the shoulder and all the lights went on in the motel. My screams were heard loud and clear. Then I knew that Hawaii was not all so wonderful. Yes, there are a few things to be cautious of, but thankfully no snakes -- they were taken care of by the mongoose who are known for their ability to kill rats, mice and snakes.

The next day was a day of looking for the usual -- housing. Our name was on the housing list at the base but in the meantime, we had to live wherever we could. Yes, we stayed at that motel for a long while. While out shopping one day I over-heard someone mention a house which would be available soon after an eviction was completed. I listened closely, got the name, ran to a lawyer, and was able to have the first chance to see it. Wow, what a mess! This was our introduction to the Ha-waiian lackadaisical lifestyle -- *Hang Loose! Relax!* This lifestyle was not a reflection on all Hawaiians -- they are great -- it's just that many have a dif-ferent approach to things.

This lovely little house had potential. I could see through the rotted wood around the sink, and even see large dead roaches under it. I had to keep reminding myself, "these are the tropics..!" I was happy to learn that our "yellow" stove was really white after a good washing, and that the two young men who were sitting on the floor playing their guitars did not stay with the property. Then great news -- the MARINES LANDED! Yes, we got some help from our marine friends to clean up the house.

I hoped we would enjoy this place for a while, but then one day I saw a man nailing a poster outside our house. The poster stated that all the houses in the cul-de-sac were to be torn down for the enlargement of the little town we were near, namely Kailua. It was quite a place, right near the ocean with warm, wonderful breezes.

So off we go -- again. At this point, I was desperate. Bill was on maneuvers, and here I am with no money and two little boys. What to do?? Thank goodness I heard a rumor that new houses were being built on Kainui Drive near the marine base. Oh, that sounded so perfect, but we were required to follow procedure to get one. First I had to join the list, which I did, and after a time, I was accepted. Then second, I had to borrow enough money for a down payment. I thank God for my sister and her husband. Yes, we finally got the house -- a lovely new ranch.

By this time Bill had returned from maneuvers and was ready to move into our lovely new ranch. Construction on the islands is a little different than it is on the mainland because of the termite problems. Our house was constructed with cedar which gave us more freedom from the bug colonies. An attached carport was built and used for our Cub Scout meetings. This was ideal, since the boys were trained in outdoor activities, and they could march and hike in the nearby hills.

From our home, we could see the Kansas Tower, the first area that was hit by the Japanese on Dec. 7, 1941. My kitchen sink faced that area which was a constant reminder of the slaughter on that day. The Arizona, which was one of the ships that was sunk during the attack, still had oil oozing up. The Pearl Harbor Memorial is placed above the sunken ship where over a thousand bodies were trapped in the hold.

Now, back to my ranch house. Grass clippings were taken from the hills and planted in rows on our land. Yes, we even had a lawn! All my plants were gifts, even the banana trees, and I could sit in my Ianai Porch and enjoy my backyard plantings knowing it was all free thanks to my good neighbors and friends.

ALOHA!

Hawaii Calls! Let Us Help You to Plan Your

TOUR to HAWAII

Jill and Bill Caldarone who have lived in Hawaii are well qualified to give you authentic island information.

Call Anytime—
HOpkins 7-9811

"Mele Kalikimaka!"

, Season's Greetings!

It was also convenient for the Cub Scout fathers to come to our home for special meetings. We remember one special trip taken with the Cubs to board a submarine at Pearl Harbor. One of the boy's fathers was in charge and received permission for us to actually go down into the submarine. This was quite memorable for all of us.

CHAPTER 9

This tour of duty happened near the end of Bill's military career. It was a sad day when we learned Bill had been transferred to Syracuse, New York and that we had to decide what to do with our ranch. We could not keep the house since we did not know what Syracuse would have to offer. Again, housing would be a problem there, too. But the house sold very quickly and though we did not make much of a profit, it was enough to buy another house in Clay, New York.

This climate change was too much for the boys. Both got sick, and we had to stay in a motel for a while. It was a miserable time for us all. Since we were expected to be in Clay for just a few months, our furniture was kept in storage and we used only the essentials.

I don't remember ever seeing roads in that area without snow cover. Rhode Island seemed like a tropical paradise compared to Syracuse. It is really too bad that I could not like the place. We had a professor who lived next door who would have enjoyed us staying. He was a lonely man who had many antique things in his barn and wanted to share them all, but I just could not do it. It was especially sad because just a short time later we were told his barn burned down and he died.

My half-empty house in Clay gave me much time to reflect on our recent adventure in Hawaii. Since there wasn't much to do and the buses got the boys to school, I had a lot of time on my hands. My recollection of one important fact was the time Bill discovered that his friend George had served on the same ship as Bill -- The Minneapolis. Most unusual. Bill spent two years of his young life (from ages 18 to 20) on board ships visiting many ports such as Guantanamo Bay, Haiti, Trinidad, The Panama Canal and of course Pearl Harbor. His ship had left Pearl Harbor just before the Japanese bombed it. We were also honored by our church to be proxy Godparents to so many children in Hawaii. All these were wonderful memories.

Korea 1950

But now back to reality. It was time for Richard's accordion lessons. This interest did not last as he was more interested in the guitar. Both he and Ronald had developed great musical talents and also had good voices, just like their Dad. He was selected to be in our graduation class to sing along with the chorus.

However, time passed and it was time to end Bill's military career. Usually, it ends with great pomp and ceremonies. Bill's departure was a little different. Because of our location, the size of the marine base, the weather, and an urgent desire to just go

Korea, 1950

home, we departed without any fanfare. Just plain ALOHA! We were glad to move "south" to Rhode island.

Wow we did it! We had survived two wars -- The Second World War and the Korean War. And by the way, the latter one almost shortened Bill's life.

The enemy was aiming to shoot Bill and one other marine in a Jeep, and this was on the day before he was scheduled to leave Korea to come home. They were able to avoid injury and death by jumping into one of the many foxholes made by his fellow marines.

CHAPTER 10

Somehow our little family survived this part of our lives. Now we faced a civilian way of life. Our biggest surprise was when Bill was told he was too old (he was just 38) for many jobs. His military pension was minimal and we had to have more income to get by. Since college was also very important for our boys, we had to seek alternative ways to improve our monetary future.

The move back to Rhode Island was quick and mostly unobserved by our family. Our thoughts were still with how quick we could adjust to a civilian way of life and leave the military behind. Somehow it seems that people were too busy to realize we were back. This took some time for us also. Jobs had to be found and our small Cape Cod house had to be refurbished since it had been rented out while we were gone. As we started slowly to get used to the feeling that we no longer had to move to the next military assignment, and the boys were going to stay in the local schools, we noticed signs in the neighborhood -- political signs. It was voting time!

Bill's service awards and medals

This brought questions about certain subjects and projects that were not done in the neighborhood. Bill made many calls which immediately got us involved in the local political scene. The first few meetings happened without a problem. But when Bill was misquoted more than once in the newspaper, we decided a political life was not for us.

CHAPTER 11

Now it was time for a diversion. Years earlier, Bill was introduced to square dancing while stationed in San Diego. During one of our military stops, we joined a group in North Carolina and enjoyed square dancing. We could not understand how these folks dancing a simple quadrille could be having so much fun -- but we soon found out. It was so revitalizing to just listen to the caller's commands and dance to the music in a group of eight people.

This was fun until we realized that we could do the same thing with our own group -- and Bill had the voice for it, too. This meant more schooling for Bill, and this time it would be Caller's Training

School. This also meant I would need to be involved because while the caller rested, typically a different type of dancing would be done -- Round Dancing -- yes, done in the round. However, it was really ballroom dancing and I would have charge of this. And this meant classes for me to learn the basics, too.

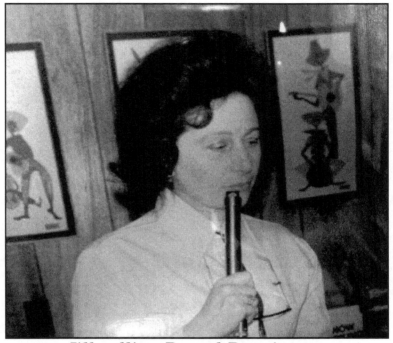

Jill calling Round Dancing

The transition was starting to take hold. But our first priority was getting our sons heading in the right direction for college. They also helped by getting part-time jobs and a loan from the military helped tremendously, too. Since Bill was told that he was too old for so many jobs, our only other alternative was to start a business of our own. Bill

JILL and BILL CALDARONE
Square, Round and Folk Dance Instructors
259 Olney Arnold Road - Cranston, R. I. 02920
Telephone 944-1880

took night school classes on real estate and appraisal work, and it helped us decide what we would do with our future.

Jill Caldarone Realty became the new name of our company. We both became brokers and hired

60

an office staff. This kept us busy, and except for calling square dances, most of our hours were spent working in real estate.

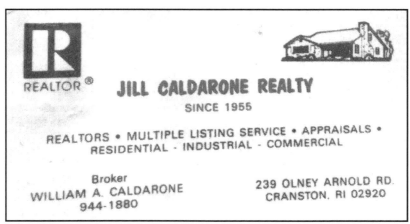

REALTOR ®

JILL CALDARONE REALTY

SINCE 1955

REALTORS • MULTIPLE LISTING SERVICE • APPRAISALS •
RESIDENTIAL - INDUSTRIAL - COMMERCIAL

Broker
WILLIAM A. CALDARONE
944-1880

239 OLNEY ARNOLD RD.
CRANSTON, RI 02920

Since time doesn't stand still, by now our sons had completed college and were ready to tend to their futures. One became a school teacher, majoring in graphic arts and the other a clinical social worker at the health department. By this time most of our families had "passed on," meaning my mom, father and many of our friends. Many of them were the people who had left their countries to come to America; some of the people never saw their parents again. So we spent time researching, seeing what they have done to come to a new country.

CHAPTER 12

Bill's father had been a tailor and a skilled barber. He also hired others to work for him. Unfortunately his mother died very young after having twelve children.

My father taught himself how to read English, drive a car (which was only a Model T at the time) and become a skilled manager in jewelry making. He was put in charge of the workers which included my sister in the office and many friends from Italy. They all had to produce, and it was such good training for all.

Today as I write this, it would be hard to concentrate on continuing our lifestyle of years ago. Since most of our friends and family have now gone, we do not have to worry about emergencies involving the weather. Right now, we happen to be experiencing the most miserable winter in many years -- snow is all we have been having. While the overall picture of snow covered trees, bushes and houses is lovely to look at, the inconvenience of it all is not. Many roofs have collapsed and there is not enough money in the city treasuries left for conditioning the roads. I wonder why Bill and I never left dear ol' Rhode for warmer climate especially since we had once lived in Hawaii? Perhaps the people are different?

CHAPTER 13

It is time to continue my story with my first born child, Richard. Richard completed many college courses and was ready for his own life. He married a lovely young lady named Mary Ann who also followed in his footsteps and became a teacher. They lived in Attleboro, Massachusetts. Life was beautiful for them, with travel and good friends until tragedy struck. Mary Ann's life was shortened by that horrible disease, cancer. This devastated us all, of course mostly Richard.

After spending some time trying to decide what to do with the rest of his life, he decided to return to Hawaii. We hated to see him go, but we knew it was best for him. He purchased land in

Kona and built a lovely new home. Later he met and married a young lady from the Philippines. They now have three beautiful children and a dog. Since there was a difference in age, Richard was concerned about the cost of education for his children as he got older. He was approached by someone who promised a financing plan from monies borrowed from the property. All the papers were checked by lawyers and it all seemed authentic, then suddenly, the balloon burst and the men took off with the money. (It was a case similar to the famous Bernie Madoff case.) Yes big problems, and maybe even foreclosures. Richard has now become quite knowledgeable in law. As of now, we still do not know what the final outcome will be but we continue to hope and pray for the best.

Our son Ronald did very well for himself, achieving all he desired in his studies, allowing him to work for the health department and later work with autistic children. He married a lovely girl also. She is a nurse who worked for group

homes helping mentally challenged children. Both
are retired now and have a lovely family -- a boy
and a girl each with children of their own.

With our boys Ronald and Richard

CHAPTER 14

It was now time for Bill and Jill to think of taking a trip. We were anxious to explore the area of Italy where our parents came from.

We had finally reached the point in our lives where we wanted to research information about our families.

First of all, we knew all our parents came from Italy. Little did we know how close our fathers lived from one another. My father was Leonardo M. from a little town in the mountains called Marzano Appio, located just about in the middle of the so-called "boot" in Italy. Bill's father happened to be born in the same town. How about that! Yes, we visited both areas where they were born.

Marzano Appio, Italy

The town is very simple -- narrow streets for small cars, ancient buildings (some have cracks in the walls from previous earthquakes), hillside plants, and cactus. Exteriors of the houses cannot be refinished since they are mostly cement work, but the interiors are lovely with plenty of marble floors, countertops and little balconies where tenants can order food from the peddlers below and have it sent up. (No elevators, just steps.) Some residents even have chickens, fireplaces are common, there is no central heating and garages are usually attached to the buildings. There are no grocery stores or meat markets except for perhaps one on or two.

Jill's family -- The Martinos

My cousin happened to have the only store and bakery in the village. It was like a department store and sold almost everything. It was also a meeting place for the village folks.

This area of Italy is also very important to chestnut growers as the climate and elevation are perfect. The size of the chestnuts are very important. They grow large and they are so delicious cooked over an open fireplace in the home. The chickens were also quite healthy; they ate leftovers -- pasta, too. And the yolks from their eggs were so rich in color.

My cousin Lucio was a college graduate and he eventually became mayor of the town. Yes, we are quite proud of him.

Bill was the first to meet him years before. His ship had anchored nearby and Bill somehow contacted Lucio (even though Bill spoke no Italian) and they managed to meet at the dock where his ship was anchored. Lucio greeted him with no car, but just a motorcycle. So here comes this marine in uniform and Lucio, on a two wheeler thing, being brought into town. Yes, it was quite the subject of conversation for the villagers. *Un Americano*!

This was the beginning of our effort to get to know our family better, especially the five children who were left behind when the Germans killed Lucio's father. There is even a monument there in memory of my uncle. Thankfully the children all went on to become successful in their own way of life. One became a nun in Rome, Lucio became mayor, Michele was a butcher, Maria worked in the grocery store with her husband (who also worked for the American military at their PX) and there was one other sibling who sadly died young. We have been to the village of Marzano Appio a few times, enough to enjoy their hospitality and customs. When I first met my cousin the nun it was during a stopover in Pompeii. The family planned a train trip to meet us just for a short time at a Pompeii restaurant. They checked our itinerary to coincide with the Pompeii stop. There were very intense feelings. My cousin looked at me and said in a meaningful tone, "*we are BLOOD related.*" Well that brought on the tears and many hugs, thinking of how our parents left their homeland to go to a strange country. We have tried very hard to keep a close relationship with them for the sake of our children. And our children are now asking questions about their family history.

They also had interesting ways of preserving their food. One day, Michele brought us deep, down into a cold dark carved out stone area in the ground, guarded by a very nasty dog. This is where they kept food like prosciutto. It was built because the Germans confiscated food when they could find it This was also called the Wine Cellars. Evidently, others in the village had the same arrangements for their food and wine.

Bill's family -- The Caldarones

While we are on that subject of food and wine, Bill and I brought my mother and Emilio back to Italy after 50 years. *Benvenuto!*

The war had demolished so many things from her home but my mother's church was still standing. She just stood still on the very alter that she had frequented when she was young, just remembering. From there we went to Venice. It was lunch time. We sat on one of the balconies in a restaurant overlooking the beautiful waterways of the city. Our thoughts were on something special for lunch. However, the waiter surprised us by suggesting something very common: *pasta e fagioli* -- beans and pasta. My mom was so surprised. This is not what she expected in such a grandiose setting. I don't remember what she finally ordered for lunch, but it certainly wasn't *pasta e fagioli*!

On another occasion when Bill and I went to Italy, we decided to go south to visit Sicily. It was so different. We had to take a ship across to the island. Lovely, beautiful Sicily! Messina is the first town on the lower part of the island, overlooking the water.

As we got closer to the top of the isle, we approached the monastery of the Capuchin Monks. The monks had a process of preserving the body after death that did not allow it to decompose completely. The corpses were separated in rows -- one row for single people, then married, then rows for other different categories. Some of the bodies were standing while others were lying down. And they still had their hair and had dried skin. They were simply amazing to look at, and really quite frightening. One little girl by the last name of "Lombardi" had been placed in a box with a see-through glass top. Her hair was blonde and she looked like she was sleeping. Her body had been there sixty years at the time we saw her. The Monks are no longer allowed to preserve bodies in this manner since the government put a stop to it. It was good to get back out into the fresh air and get away from the smell of death.

So further up the isle we went and saw much in between. Sicily is noted for the grapes they grow and the wines that are produced and sent all over the world. A particular grape grown in the higher and cooler area is called *Nero d'Avola*.

We arrived at the top of the island at a place called Taormina. It was really colorful. There were little, brightly painted push carts, a sports arena, and all sorts of activities were happening. Their ice cream was a big attraction, too. And since it was a warm day, we stopped for a special scoop. This was when we noticed that men were always the first to be served, and never the women. How about that?!

After a very interesting visit, we started the trip down toward the ferry that would take us back to the mainland. Before that, however, not to be forgotten, we visited Mt. Etna. Yes, we did go to see it. It is colder as you approach the volcano and there is always the threat of an eruption.

As for the language, it seems that the Sicilians add more to the words than the other Italian dialects. Most areas of Italy from Milan on down have their own distinct way of using the Italian language. I remember we had a landlady once who was Sicilian. The Sicilians are a very hard working people; one of her sons became a lawyer another a teacher. But her language is something I never could understand.

She also tried pulling my tonsils out with a handful of salt! All I remember was her running out screaming because I bit her, not allowing her to do what she meant to do as well intentioned as it was. We called her Zia Pippina. This happened when I was very young.

As for the volcanoes, how about the disaster at Pompeii!? It's amazing to imagine the area being burned out with hot volcanic ash. They still have things on display that were found from all those years ago; things like a loaf of bread, dogs, and even people seem still intact. It happened so suddenly that people could not escape the catastrophe. Their gardens, homes and roads are still there, buried, and now it's hard to imagine that people ever used to inhabit the area at all.

As I mentioned, my son still lives on the big Island of Hawaii where there is an active volcano. This however continues to enlarge the island with the lava cooling as it goes out to into the sea.

CHAPTER 15

But it is now time to settle down in little ol' Rhode Island. There is much to see and discover in our little state. First of all, we have the ocean. I learned to appreciate that when we had the house on the shoreline in Warwick. I remember the mornings were so quiet and peaceful whether the tide was low or high. The house was protected by Narragansett Bay not the ocean front, and things were a little more tranquil because of the location. I remember the little crabs trying to dodge everything, and at low tide we could see many of them. Periwinkles were in abundance, too; they were so good to eat with a little tomato sauce. Back then all this so-called cooking was done on kerosene stoves. We had no gas connections in those days. Plus, we used an outdoor "john;" there was no plumbing either. Then once a month during the full moon, the tide would embrace the area.

Well, we all survived all our relocations through the years and had a great time while it lasted. When we finally returned to Rhode Island to stay, much had to be done to refurbish our little Cape Cod style home. This and our so-called "little activities" took up much of our time. As I mentioned, we got very involved in this thing called square dancing, and created a square dance and round dance club which of course meant we had to attend many meetings. We also had to create some way to make money and pay our bills, and that's when we decided to start Jill Caldarone Realty.

Yet somehow we still found time to be in parades, enjoy dancing, work with the mentally and physically challenged for 17 years, and program dancing and singing. And in my spare time, I became a Master Gardener (I was inducted into the Master Gardener Hall of Fame at the University of Rhode Island) and founded two different garden clubs.

Gardening club memories.

And now we are almost at the time in our lives where we may want to just relax and enjoy the family and grandchildren...

... and perhaps

... take another trip to Hawaii?

I do hope you have enjoyed being with us --
Bill and Jill from Federal Hill -- for this little so-
journ. So until we meet again...

Aloha! And the best to all!

~ Bill and Jill

ABOUT THE AUTHOR

Pictured here with former Rhode Island Governor and Mrs. Don Carcieri at their 70th wedding anniversary in 2014, Bill and Jill Caldarone have been married since 1944 and still reside in Cranston, RI.

Made in the USA
Middletown, DE
23 July 2016